CW00872128

SIMPLE MACHINES

MARLA CONN

rourke
Educational Media

A Division of
Carson
Dellosa
Education

rourkeeducationalmedia.com

Photo Glossary

 **bottle cap**

 **cart**

 **fishing pole**

 ramp

 seesaw

 zipper

A **ramp** is a simple machine.

ramp

A **zipper** is a simple machine.

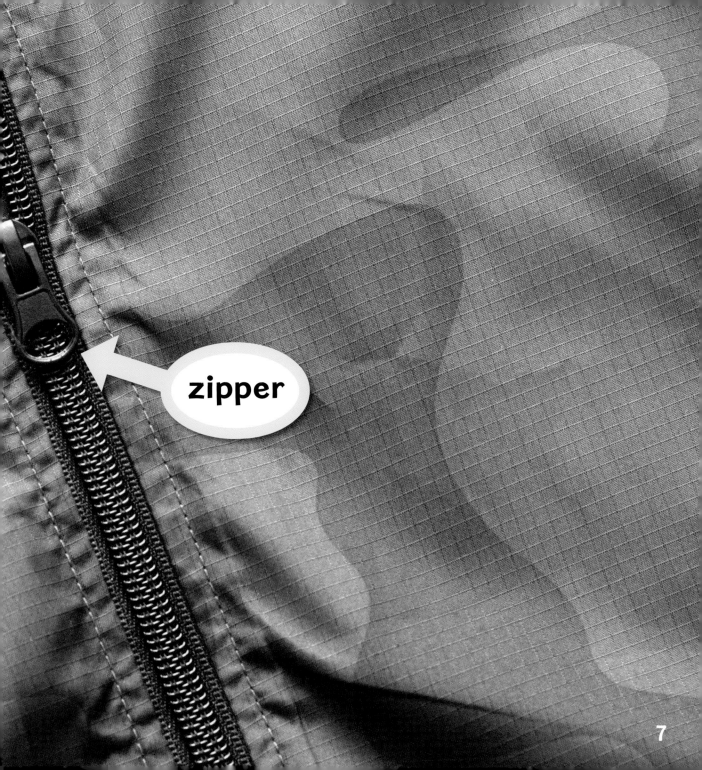

zipper

A **bottle cap** is a simple machine.

bottle cap

A **seesaw** is a simple machine.

A **cart** is a simple machine.

cart

A **fishing pole** is a simple machine.

fishing pole

15

Activity

1. Make a list of all of the objects from the book and tell how they help you.

2. Look at the pictures of types of simple machines below and discuss.

3. Match the types of simple machines below to the simple machines in the book.

4. Think of other things around your home or school that are simple machines.

   - Screw
   - Wheel & axel
   - Inclined plane
   - Wedge
   - Lever
   - Pulley